A GIFT FROM GOD

Taste Him Through Poetry

Phoenix Joi

Published in USA by Trinity Publishing Company

Paperback ISBN: 978-1-969749-39-1

Table of Contents

Dedication

This book is dedicated to those who don't know God or are unsure of His magnificence. Through these poetic glimpses, may you experience just a small taste of His goodness.

Introduction

There are moments in life when we wonder who God is, what He's like, and whether He truly sees us. Some grew up hearing about His power and His love, while others are still searching, unsure, curious, or quietly hoping for something real. Wherever you find yourself, this book offers just a taste—enough for your heart to sense the goodness of God for yourself.

These poems come from personal reflections, quiet prayers, and the many ways God reveals Himself in everyday life. Through His comfort, His guidance, His peace, and His gentle voice, He reminds us that He is always present and always good. Each poem is a glimpse of moments where faith grew stronger and His presence became unmistakable.

My hope is that as you read, you'll feel Him draw close to you too—not through perfect words, but through the simple truth that His love is real, His power is great, and His goodness can be experienced by anyone who seeks Him.

Welcome to *A Taste of God*. May these pages inspire your spirit and nourish your soul.

He Walks Beside Us

A faithful friend who's with you till the end—
You never have to explain things to Him.
He has the answer, the solution to every problem or issue;
All we have to do is trust Him.

Stand still and know that He is God—watch Him work.

Whether preacher or teacher,

Parent, congregation, student, or child,
Everyone is the same in His eyes;

No one greater than the next.

To follow Him is the greatest thing that can ever be done.
Trusting Him is receiving the richest man's inheritance.

Provider, Comforter, Healer, Counselor—whatever we need.
He's on time,

A Keeper, the calm before and after a storm.

He walks beside us.

Perfect Guide

On a journey, unsure which way to go—
To follow the advice of friends and family,
Or a feeling that hits—
Just stand.

Remembering childhood and adolescence,
Your eyes close, and a prayer begins:

Dear God, here I am, humble and sorry.
I know I'm not where You want me.
I ask You now to guide my footsteps.
I surrender, Son of God.
It's You I want to be like.

Teach me Your ways; mine hurt me.
The good I do not see.
Earlier in life I was told You are perfect.
I ask You now, will You be my guide?

A feeling comes over you—
Your life is changed forever.

Magnificent Doctor

No stethoscope, prescription, or medication—
He knows the body better than anyone.
Every ouch, pain, and stomachache,
He knows why—and how to get rid of it.

No X-rays, tests, or blood draws;
He can fix it and never misdiagnoses.
The best Surgeon there is or ever will be,
He can heal on the spot or while we sleep.

No anesthesia necessary—
Just relax, breathe in.
Sometimes, He will work through a doctor.

He's a wonderful wonder.

Faith Increase

For as long as I can remember, I knew You.
I was told long ago of Your miraculous power.

You turned water into wine,
Gave sight to the blind,
Gave the lame their steps—
Caught my attention.

When I was born, two weeks was my life span,
But You said, "Live on."
Thank You, Lord Jesus,
For all You did and allowed me to do.

Going through school and becoming a Who's Who in college,
Many things I saw and people I met—
I'm amazed at what I see.
Some things are unexplainable;
All the glory goes to You.

You spoke to me in my time of need,
A voice so soft and calm,
Answering questions,
Telling me what would happen.

"Ask, and I shall receive."
This Word proves true.

It's Mine

Name it, claim it, believe it.
Praying for some goals to be met,
If it's God's will—
Not realizing they're already done.

He knew what was needed long before we did.
It was in His plan, even what we want—
No bad or evil wants.

Mention it. Look—it's in front of us.
Sometimes we just think it.

When we receive, we say, "It's mine."
If we have to wait longer,
Or gain added strength—mental, physical—
Not to get weak,
But to show sincerity.

We pray in Jesus' name,
Gathering more strength.
Anything asked in My name shall be given,
Knowing—it's mine.

Clean Up

In Your hands, You see my spirit—
the potential I have to bring others to You.

I was sent to earth to grow and mature,
Beginning in my mother's womb.

As I grew older, I began to stray,
Turning left when You told me to stay right.
Worldly temptations took over,
Yet I still felt Your gentle touch.

I fell to my knees and cried,
"Please forgive me, Father.
Take me back to when I first received You.
Wash me and cleanse me afresh.
I surrender—I am Yours."

You guided my spirit back.
My words became what You gave me.

Thank You, God,
For still seeing me fit to be cleaned up.

Paid in Full

Without a word He was tortured

Starved beaten bruised and whipped

Son of GOD unrecognizable.

He had a heart to save future generations

 Even those He didn't know

 He was nailed to a cross and further tortured.

Father forgive them

For they know not what they do was said.

Jesus died He paid for us

He saw the worth of you and me.

He rose again and gave us a choice

I choose to follow Thee

King of kings Lord of lord.

Lean On You

Bodies grow tired from the activities of the day, yet call Your name.
At each sound of Your name, energy returns.

When we are weak, You show Your strength.

Lord Jesus, let me lean on You.
Feeling Your touch, Your gentle pull saying, "Lean on Me."

A soft pillow, softer than any other, is under my head — the Lord's shoulder.
His soft voice says, "I will give you rest."

Many people can need Him at once;

He always has room and never tires.

Right Here

I won't be scared.

Through life's journey God is with me.
Nor quiver when You whisper in my ear.
When I'm feeling weak,

You sprinkle down strength.

But God, You're so magnificent — helping was already in the plan.
Above all bad and evil, You hold me in Your right hand of righteousness.

Right here, taking on my battles.

Season to Season

Seasons change

Summer to fall,

Fall to winter,

Winter to spring,

Spring to summer,

And back again.

People and personalities do as well.

The Word and love of God never will;
It is forever settled in Heaven.

The weather changes all the time.
The whisper and calmness of God's voice will not.
He is the same yesterday, today, and forever.

Thank You, Jesus!

"Let this cup pass from Me;

Nevertheless, Father, Your will be done."

Jesus knew a huge task had to be done.

Being beaten, bruised, whipped beyond recognition —
This represents the sin we commit.

Nailed to the cross He carried it.
Jesus told God to forgive them.
Have pity on us;
They know not what they do.

He gave His life, then was placed in a sepulcher.
The third day Jesus rose — resurrection.

Thank You, Jesus!

This started a new life.
No sign of sin.
He was born again.

When I Wake

When I wake
Before the noise
Before the schedule
Before the world asks anything of me.

I breathe
And remember
I am not alone.

God is already awake
Already watching
Already making a way.

I stretch my faith
Along with my arms
And say thank You
For another chance to try again.

When I wake
Hope is fresh
Mercy is new
And grace is already waiting

That's a good way to start the day.

Sunday Morning Breakfast

The house smells like coffee
And something warm in the oven
Sunlight peeks through the window
Like it's in on the blessing.

Pajamas still on
Hair not quite ready for church
But my heart already is.

Plates clink softly
Laughter settles at the table
Grace is said slowly
So everyone can hear.

God sits with us
Right between the syrup and the smiles
No rush
No pressure
Just presence.

Sunday morning breakfast
Feels like heaven practiced early.

He Is Great

He is great
Not just in the big things
But in the small
Quiet moments I almost miss.

Great when doors open
And just as great when they don't
Great in miracles
And even greater in mercy.

He holds the world steady
Yet still listens when I whisper
That kind of greatness
Deserves my praise.

So I lift my hands
Even when my words are simple
Because He doesn't need fancy
He just needs my heart.

Yes!
He is great
And that is more than enough.

Anchored in His Voice

The world has opinions
Lots of them
Loud ones
Helpful ones
And some I didn't request.

But Your voice
Is steady
Like an anchor that doesn't move
Even when everything else does.

You don't shout over the noise
You simply wait
Until I lean in close enough to hear.

You say
"Stay right here"
When I want to rush ahead
You say
"Trust Me"
When I start overthinking.

And somehow
That's enough.

Your voice doesn't rush me
Doesn't pressure me
Doesn't confuse me.

It calms
It grounds
It reminds me who I am.

So when the world gets busy
And my thoughts try to run the show
I listen for You,

Because peace always sounds like Your voice.

A Vessel Still Saying Yes

I told You yes once
A long time ago
And I'm still learning
What that yes really means

It means showing up
Even when I'm tired
It means listening
Even when I'd rather talk

It means being open
Available
And occasionally surprised
By where You lead

Some days I say yes confidently
Other days it's more like
"Yes, Lord… but can we talk about this?"

Still
You smile
And use me anyway

I don't have to be perfect
I just have to be willing

So here I am again
Hands open
Heart ready

A vessel
Still learning
Still growing
Still saying yes

And somehow
That's enough for You.

I Hear You, Lord

I hear You, Lord
Even when I pretend I don't
Like when You say rest
And I say just five more minutes.

You speak softly
Not in thunder
But in nudges
And reminders I didn't ask for.

You say turn left
I lean right
Then pause
Because somehow You're still right.

You whisper slow down
I speed up
You smile patiently
Waiting for me to catch on.

I hear You when You say forgive
And I sigh deeply
Because I already practiced my argument.

I hear You say trust Me
When I want the plan
The details
And a backup plan.

Still
You stay gentle

Never rushing
Never raising Your voice.

Just steady
Just kind
Just there.

So yes, Lord
I hear You
Eventually.

And when I do
Life seems lighter
My steps make sense
And peace shows up right on time.

Thanks for speaking
Even when I'm distracted
You're really good at getting my attention.

When God Whispered Strength

I came to You carrying questions
Heavy with the sound of my own doubt
Wondering if You still heard me
After all the times I cried in silence.

But You were there
Closer than my fear
Counting every tear
Calling each one by name.

You walked with me in the good days
And stayed when the road went dark
When I didn't know which way was forward
You became my direction.

Insecurity tried to speak louder
Told me I was fragile
Unqualified
Not enough.

But You interrupted the noise
And gently said
That weakness was not my identity
It was the place where You would show up.

You whispered into the ache of my heart
"I am Strength!"

And suddenly I stood taller
Not because I was fearless
But because You were faithful.

You told me to ask
And reminded me I had already received
Victory was never waiting ahead
It was placed within me long ago.

So I stay forgiven, grounded, held,

Strong, not by my power,
But by the voice that called me His.

Built by Grace, Not by Fear

I open my ears so I can hear You
Not the world's demands
Not yesterday's regrets
But Your steady voice calling me forward.

I open my eyes to see what You see
Not what distracts
Not what deceives
But what aligns me with Your truth.

Take me back
To the moment I first said yes
When belief was simple
And surrender was full.

Fill me
Lead me
Take control
I am not here to be impressive
I am here to be a vessel.

I follow You day by day
Even when the world is loud
Even when everything around me pulls
I choose not to let it in.

Because grace has built something in me
Fear never could.

You taught me how to walk steady
How to trust without needing proof
How to stand firm without hardening my heart.

Everything You are doing
Everything You have already done
Has carried me here.

So I lift my thanks
And lay down my pride
Your glory above all else.

You are first
You are constant
You are enough.

And I am built—
By grace
Not by fear.

Life With God

He's a wonderful friend,

Never too busy and can lend an ear to listen.

The best Father you can ever have,

Always by your side.

He teaches the right way to go.

Happen to go your own way,

He doesn't hold it over your head.
God stays beside you,

Pick you up and turns you around.

Sickness, pain —

That's no problem.

God's a doctor.
With the slightest little faith.

A word or a touch from God — that's lifted.

Get into an emotional battle, get tempted or unsure,

Just tell Him.
Be still, know the battle is won.

Struggling

Come to Me, I'm right here.
Lord, I'm in trouble, don't know what to do.

Take My yoke upon you.
Things got so hard for me.

My yoke is easy.
Stress is a burden weighing me down.

I will give you rest.
All your burdens for Mine.

My burden is light.

Delivery

A companion, someone to share life with, there when scared.
Seek God first — the ultimate Father and Counselor.

His righteousness is never wrong.
He'll deliver what is asked, sometimes a little more.

Right on time.

I'm His

"Touch not My anointed, do My prophets no harm,"
I hear God say when I'm scared.

I feel Him surrounding me until fear goes bye.
I don't know where I would be — I would be and could do nothing without
the Lord.

My strength is gained from day to day.
My Protector from pain or bad thoughts — they come but cannot stay.

I ask His forgiveness, and He does,
And never brings it up again.

He's a man who cannot lie, neither does He repent,
Whose Word is good now and forever.

Pain taunting me — my Lord says enough.
Pain runs away fast, emotionally and physically.

"Touch not My anointed, do My prophet no harm,"
Said the Man who died for and saved me,
Showing me my worth.

Thank You, Jesus — yes, I'm His.

Victorious

Hold me, Lord, so I know You're there.
Guide my footsteps; I want to follow You.

Whisper in my ear so that we can talk.
Your voice, so sweet but powerful, will keep me from trouble.

If I should happen to get in,
With You, I have victory.

Counselor

Tears fall as waterfalls for an event that shouldn't have ended.
A smiling face instead of stress was the result of talks.

Waterfalls turn into a peaceful river;
A soft whisper is heard.

A soft touch — the tears stop,
A sense of peace takes over.

No need to explain; I already know.
"I will wipe every tear from your eyes."

Praise

Oh Lord my God, I know that I'm not worthy, but You say I am.
Before I was here, You put my sins on Your shoulders and were crucified for me.

Lord Jesus, You suffered and died.
Though I mess up and hurt You again and again, all You require is repentance.
Then You wash and cleanse me once again.

I surrender to You, my Savior — hold me,

Guide me down Your path.
You gave me a gift, Your Holy Spirit, the Comforter, to guide me through life.

With a book, the Bible, let me know my life isn't a surprise—You understand.

I lift my hands to You; I surrender and praise Your name

Thank You for knowing me.
I will pray in Your name —

You hear me and You care

Father God, You knew and had a plan before I entered my mother.
I will be a follower of You and Your Son, Jesus Christ.

Stand

Tears fall as waterfalls,
As thoughts enter the mind—
Some controllable,
Others not.

Rebuking every thought,
Asking the Lord forgiveness and help.

"Touch not My anointed;
Do My prophet no harm"
Enters the mind.

A gentle feeling—
Arms wrap around,
Troubled thoughts leave,
Tears clear.

This battle is won.
Thank You, Lord.

Sometimes don't move,
Just stand.

Give It to Me

"Come to Me, all that labor tirelessly;
I will give you rest."
I'm the Provider.

Every burden, worry—
Share them with Me;
I can take the weight.

Peace is what I give.
Your deepest cares are Mine,
For I care for you.

I'm the Keeper.

With each step, I am there with you,
Even when you feel alone.

I am a Keeper
Who wants to lead your way.

Everything you're going through, and feeling,
I've been there before.

This God has been tested and tried.

Give Me every problem,
Burden, worry—
I will trade them, giving you peace.

The promises of the Lord your God
Never change.
He is the ultimate Comforter.

Get Thee Behind

God's soldier was under attack,
Yet never did he lose faith in the Lord.

Time to put war clothes on—
The armor of God.

The helmet of salvation,
Shown every day.

Something bringing those he tells together:
The sword of the Spirit.

They stop what they're doing
To pray.

The breastplate of righteousness,
Giving him humbleness and understanding.

When people see him calm,
He is very peaceful.

Now is the time to get behind him, Satan,
While friends and loved ones pray and praise,

Stomping on your head.

Help Lord

Hard times come around that could change life forever

Scary issues hit but how to fix them is uncertain

The perfect time to pray

Lord open my ears that I may hear you my eyes that I may see what you want to see

I'm right here a soft whisper says then gives an answer

Seek me and you will find me.

Weak

The joy of the Lord is my strength

Words of encouragement and truth

When the torment discouragement and stress show up let good thoughts pull back

Laughter end good is just like medicine, strength is returning

The joy of the Lord is your strength.

Ultimate Love

Heavenly Father, you knew me before I knew me and I would need help

You sacrificed your son Jesus for me, and did it without a doubt

He carried my sins along with the cross up Calvary

Died and rose again sending me a Comforter an advocate to lead and guide me

Showing me my worth, you call me your child

I get in trouble seen and unseen you tell me stand still the battle is yours

When I mess up, I repent you forgive and remember my sins no more

Thank you for your grace and renewed mercy every morning

Love I don't even have to ask for or deserve

Ultimate love.

The Promise Land

This grassy plain filled with trees, houses and animals is not home
But a rest stop with things that can disappear as fast as the drop of a hat
Where sickness and pain are a common place
And killing is no stranger
This is just a pit stop to the home God promised.

A place where streets are of gold not plated but pure
And gates of pearl, each having its own individual purpose
 A land filled with jewels of purpose but gold not only for streets
All of this incorruptible, houses indisputable.

In this land no more tears of sadness: sickness and pain are not welcome
Disability and missing body parts are no more - everybody made perfect
Homelessness, well that's gone to a mansion put in its place
And everything that is needed is always pure
No fighting nor killing just praising and worshiping
Not even darkness the glory and Jesus are the light
There's a glimpse of the Promise Land, home.

My House

God made me who I am—
The One who formed me,
The One who knows me.

My house is perfect,
For I am fearfully
And wonderfully made.

My house was shaped by His hands,
Filled with His breath,
Held up by His Word.

He guards every door,
Covers every room,
Walks the hallways of my heart.

The world may see flaws,
But God calls it good.

This house—
His creation—
Stands because of Him.

Kept by His Hand

Many storms could have taken me,
But His hand held me still.

Winds blew,
Waves rose,
Fear tried to speak—
But God whispered louder.

"Peace, be still,"
And my heart obeyed.

I didn't make it on my own;
I was kept, carried, and covered.

Every day I rise
Is proof of His goodness.
Kept by His hand—
I am safe.

His Voice

In the quiet moments
When my thoughts grow heavy,
I hear Him.

Not loud,
Not demanding—
Just a soft voice
That settles everything.

"You're Mine.
Don't be afraid."

And suddenly
The questions fade,
The weight lifts,
Peace settles in.

His voice
Is the place
My soul rests.

Always Enough

When I felt empty,
He filled me.

When strength was gone,
He became it.

When hope dimmed,
He spoke light.

Every place of "not enough"
Became more than enough
In His hands.

God never runs out—
Not of mercy,
Not of patience,
Not of love.

And because He is enough,
I am held.

I Belong to Him

Before I understood love,
He loved me.

Before I knew purpose,
He called me.

Before I reached for Him,
He reached for me first.

Every blessing,
Every breath,
Every moment of grace
Whispers the same truth:

I belong to Him.
Not by accident,
Not by chance—
But by His choosing.

And because I am His,
I am home.

My Keeper

Open my ears, that I may hear You—
My eyes, that I may see
What You desire for me to see.

I see myself in visions,
My faith in Thee increasing.

Take me back to where I first received You,
When nothing distracted me
From what You spoke to my heart.

Your vessel was all I longed to be.
In Your arms,
Hearing Your voice,
I found rest.

A Promise from the Ultimate

What we say could be intentional or fake.

When the Lord speaks, never fake—always take.

He holds it higher than His name.

God's will be done; He had a plan

Before we were born,

For each of us individually.

In Jesus' name, God's will be done.

A simple prayer, nothing evil.

Ask, and you shall receive—sometimes immediately,

Right in time for others.

If it's meant to be,

It will be.

Made Me Strong

Someone told me, You are here and hear my every cry.
You see every tear; in every heartbreak,
it's been You by my side.

You guide my footsteps in the good times,
even when I don't know which way to go.
When insecurity had hold of me,
You replaced it with confidence.

Lord, You helped me understand
that *this* is weakness.
Then You calmly whispered in my ear,
"I am Strength."

I will stay with You, my Lord—I need You.
God, please forgive my wrongs.
You said, *Ask and you shall receive.*
You have already made me strong.
I have victory.

The Connection to Christ

Open my ears that I may hear,
my eyes that I may see
what You want me to see.

Take me back to when I first received Thee.
Fill my body; take control—
I am Your vessel.

Speak, lead me; I'll follow,
a sincere follower day by day.
Though I see earthly activity around me,
I will not let it get in my way.

Everything You are doing
and everything You have done—
thank You.
Glory to Your name.
You are always number one.

The Son Always Shines

God's Word turned human form
To show us the way.

Pure, sin-free from day to day.

Though trials come,
He never held anger,
But walked away or forgave.

Anger, but sin not—
That's the way to be.

Follow the One
Who took on our sins
And gave His life.

Now He is the Light.

Follow Him
Down the right path.

Anointed One

(Just a little about Ada J. Gotcher, whom God called Phoenix Joi.)

"Touch not My anointed,
Do My prophet no harm."

A fit in Your hand—
Preemie born at the start of the year.
She had a disability
That didn't hurt her helpful personality.

A God-given gift
Led her down the path of tutoring awhile,
Trying a few subjects,
But a passion for English and writing confirmed.

In the late teenage years,
Seizures came—
It was October 31st.
Waking up a few seconds later
To find herself in the ambulance
Is what's remembered.

What Satan meant for evil,
God turned around for good.
You see, amongst all her other writing,
Now she writes for the Lord as well.

"Touch not My anointed,
Do My prophet no harm."

This strengthened her faith.
Born four months premature,
A baby fit for the palm of the hand.
Talking at nine months—
Expectation defied.

Two weeks of life

Turned to thirty-seven years and beyond.
A special gift,
A college graduate,
And who knows how much more.

Author Bio

She was born Ada Gotcher, but as she matured, she answered God's call and embraced the name Phoenix—a symbol of rebirth, purpose, and divine transformation.

Born four months premature on January 26, 1988, at just 3 pounds 8 ounces, Phoenix Joi entered the world as a living testimony of strength. Raised by her parents, Cheryl and George, in a small Texas town, she began school at age two and quickly fell in love with stories. From *Goodnight Moon* and *The Cat in the Hat* to the *American Girl* series and *Nancy Drew* mysteries, books became her earliest companions.

By age eleven, life brought challenges she struggled to express. Her mother gently placed a pen and paper in her hand and encouraged her to write. That moment sparked her lifelong connection to words. With an active imagination, Phoenix first experimented with short stories, then discovered her love of poetry during a school unit that introduced her to Emily Dickinson. Poetry became her outlet—her voice when spoken words felt too heavy.

Her gift began to shine publicly in middle school when she was asked to write a poem for the Black History program. Unsure how it would be received, she was humbled by the overwhelming response. From then on, she wrote poems to express apologies, appreciation, friendship, and even love.

After her grade school years ended, God redirected her writing toward His glory. Her first faith-centered poem, Strength, marked a turning point. Through surgeries, hardships, silent battles, and moments of deep struggle, Phoenix experienced the transforming power of Jesus Christ. His forgiveness, protection, and constant presence became her anchor and the heartbeat of her poetry.

Phoenix continued her education with determination. She earned her Associate's degree from Paris Junior College and later attended East Texas State University to pursue her Bachelor's degree. Though she did not complete the program, her time there strengthened her love of learning and her passion for English and writing.

Today, Phoenix Joi writes to honor God, share His goodness, and remind others of His unwavering love. Each poem reflects her journey—a testimony of resilience and faith in the God who rescued, restored, and called her His own.

Her life and her writing proclaim one truth:
God is still strengthening, shaping, and elevating her—day by day.

Acknowledgments

I would like to express my deepest gratitude to my mother for placing a pen in my hand and giving me a healthy outlet during some of my most difficult moments. Her guidance fostered my creativity and shaped me into the writer I am today.

I am grateful to my schools for providing opportunities to share my creative work and for fostering an environment where my imagination could grow. Through a poetry unit in school, I discovered that poetry came more easily to me than general writing. That experience also helped me recognize poetry as a gift from God.

To my dad, who always said my love of poetry came from him—thank you. I honor and acknowledge that influence.

To my church family, thank you for inspiring many of the poems in this book and for continually encouraging me to write. Your support has meant more than you know.

A special thank you to my cousin, Erica Spencer, for connecting me with a publisher willing to partner with me on this journey.

To my family and friends, thank you for keeping me encouraged and reminding me to keep writing.

And finally, Trinity Writing and Publishing—thank you for working with me and helping bring this book to life.

www.ingramcontent.com/pod-product-compliance
Lightning Source LLC
LaVergne TN
LVHW051210080426
835512LV00019B/3190